# VISION RETREAT
## GUIDEBOOK

*Establishing a Yearly Vision for Your Marriage & Family*

# JIMMY & KAREN EVANS

*Vision Retreat Guidebook*
*Establishing a Yearly Vision for Your Marriage & Family*

First edition published January 1, 2008 by MarriageToday™ as
*Mountaintop of Marriage: A Vision Retreat Guidebook*

Copyright ©2021 by XO Publishing.

ISBN: 978-1-950113-59-0 (Paperback)
ISBN: 978-1-950113-60-6 (eBook)

P.O. Box 59888 Dallas, Texas 75229
1-800-380-6330
or visit our website at www.xomarriage.com

XO Publishing

*Printed in the United States of America*

# CONTENTS

# INTRODUCTION

## Moving Forward...Together

*Come, and let us go up to the mountain of the LORD...*
*He will teach us His ways and we shall walk in His paths.*

MICAH 4:2 NKJV

Early in his career as a pastor, my dad found himself feeling overwhelmed. He was leading a rapidly growing church and, as he describes it, didn't really feel equipped for the challenges of ministry. So he immersed himself in books about leadership. Several authors kept highlighting the importance of vision, and one verse they each pointed to was Proverbs 29:18: *Where there is no vision, the people perish.*

These leadership and church growth experts taught that vision keeps an organization or a team unified. With a goal before them, a group of people could set their focus and move together in the right direction. It's good leadership advice! But if you know Jimmy Evans—and his story—you won't be surprised to know that eventually he began thinking of that verse outside the context of church growth.

Could the need for vision also apply to marriage?

In the original Hebrew, the word we translate *perish* has a deeper meaning. It means "unrestrained." Think about two people who are tied together. When two are restrained but try to do their own thing, they pull against each other. They go in circles. They fight. They struggle to move in the same direction *unless* they work in tandem. They need to agree upon an established direction—in other words, they need a "vision"—and only then can they actually move forward.

A husband and wife are already linked together, but their marriage needs a purpose. They need a vision.

Around the same time, my dad had a conversation with a pastor friend in another state. The pastor mentioned that he and his wife were getting ready to go on their annual "vision retreat." That was the first time my dad had heard those words. He asked the friend to tell him more.

The pastor explained that he and his wife had made a practice of getting away together, for four or five days every year, to make sure they were on the same page regarding their goals, priorities and values. In other words, they spent a few days seeking God and allowing Him to refine a vision for their marriage.

As my dad explains it, this served as a lightbulb moment for him and his ministry. He had already been thinking that a husband and wife needed a direction, and a vision retreat seemed to be the perfect strategy for getting away together, seeking God, and figuring out what exactly that direction was. He and my mom planned their first vision retreat that same year.

It transformed their relationship. Their marriage was already good going into it, but they left it having reached a new level of intimacy and purpose. In the years since, they've invested time each year for a private vision retreat for just the two of them.

On multiple occasions, I've heard him tell audiences it is one of the most powerful and productive things a husband and wife can do for their marriage and family. He's right. In our own marriage, Stephanie and I have spent several years following that example. Words can't express how meaningful these times are, not just in drawing us closer together but in helping us discover who we are and what God has planned for us.

As often as my dad teaches about this topic, Stephanie and I also find ourselves encouraging our own friends about the benefits of a vision retreat. Together, all of us have identified some of the most important elements and practices of this special time for a husband and wife. The purpose of this guidebook is to share these steps with you. For the sake of your marriage, we encourage you to schedule a vision retreat of your own, making use of this resource.

As you embark on this journey, please take your time to talk about and think through the questions that follow. Answer them together! While not every question or topic may apply to your specific situation, it is our prayer that you'll follow this process and allow God to use it to transform your marriage.

— Brent Evans

# ANSWERS TO FREQUENTLY ASKED QUESTIONS

We know you already have questions about the purpose and execution of a vision retreat. Let's get those out of the way first. Here are our answers to some of the typical questions we get.

**Do we have to go away to have a vision retreat? Can't we just have one at home?**
Where you "retreat" doesn't matter. What matters most is that you can get away from everyday life. However, we've found that this is difficult to do at home, where you're subject to any number of distractions: kids, phones, household tasks, and everything else. By definition, a retreat is a period of time removed from familiar activities or surroundings. You don't have to go far, but it's definitely helpful to get away.

**Does a vision retreat have to be expensive?**
Not at all! It doesn't have to be at a luxury resort or an exotic locale (though that's certainly fine if it's an option for you). If you don't want to go far, it can be just as effective to book a hotel or Airbnb in your own town. The important thing is to get alone together, listen to God, and talk.

**How long should a vision retreat be?**
We've found that at least two or three days is ideal. While it is possible to make a lot of progress in a single day—and while any amount of time is better than none at all—you really need at least two days and nights alone to make your way through this guide.

**Can we take our children?**
Please don't! It may feel like too much of a luxury to make arrangements for your kids while you're gone. It may even make you feel guilty! But the best thing you can do for your children is to cultivate a strong marriage. That's what you're doing with your vision retreat.

**Can we have fun? Do we have to spend all our time locked in a room?**

Fun should be a priority! Be as active as you want. Plan a romantic, relaxing and invigorating few days together. Recreation and entertainment should be key elements of your time away.

**What should we take with us?**

Other than destination-appropriate clothing, bring your Bible, something to write with, and this guidebook. Most importantly, bring a sense of anticipation that God will meet you on your retreat and work in your hearts.

**Are there any videos to accompany this guidebook?**

We wrote this book to stand alone, but if this is your first time doing the vision retreat or if you want to dive deeper, consider checking out the bonus videos available on XO Now. In these videos, Jimmy Evans guides you through the entire vision retreat, step by step. While these videos aren't required, they are designed to help you through each phase of your vision retreat journey. Find the videos at xomarriage.com/visionvideos

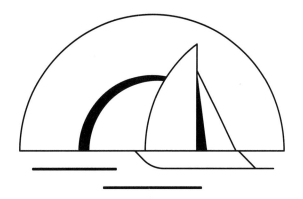

# PREPARATION

## Do These Things Before You Go...

**Pray**

Several weeks or days before your retreat, begin asking God to prepare your spirit for this time together. Pray as a couple but also pray as individuals. Ask for clear eyes and soft hearts. Surrender to Him and ask Him to reveal any areas where your relationship can improve.

**List**

When those areas become clear, write them here.

(HIM) Things I need to work on:
*(examples: communication, listening, respect, romance...)*

_____

_____

_____

(HER) Things I need to work on:
*(examples: communication, listening, respect, romance...)*

_____

_____

_____

(HIM) Things our relationship needs:
*(examples: more date nights, more time together, more conversation...)*

_____

_____

_____

(HER) Things our relationship needs:
*(examples: more date nights, more time together, more conversation...)*

_____

_____

_____

(HIM) Conflicts we need to resolve:
*(tip: list specific areas of disagreement in your marriage)*

_____

_____

_____

(HER) Conflicts we need to resolve:
*(tip: list specific areas of disagreement in your marriage)*

_____

_____

_____

(HIM) Topics we need to discuss:
*(tip: list specific topics related to your marriage)*

_____

_____

_____

(HER) Topics we need to discuss:
*(tip: list specific topics related to your marriage)*

_____

_____

_____

**Love**

Think about what you love most about your spouse. Each of you write down five things you love or appreciate about the other.

(HIM) 5 reasons I love her:

1. _____

2. _____

3. _____

4. _____

5. _____

(HER) 5 reasons I love him:

1. _____

2. _____

3. _____

4. _____

5. _____

## Rate

Consider the current intimacy of your marriage before the retreat. Not just physical intimacy, but emotional and spiritual intimacy. Each of you rate the state of your marriage.

HIM: I rate the intimacy and closeness of our marriage as…

**Less Intimate**                                    **More Intimate**

1        2        3        4        5        6        7        8        9        10

HER: I rate the intimacy and closeness of our marriage as…

**Less Intimate**                                    **More Intimate**

1        2        3        4        5        6        7        8        9        10

**Get Ready**

On your vision retreat, it will be vital for the two of you to communicate. You will have to talk, even if it's not your nature or temperament to do so. Go into your time together already committed to opening up with each other.

# PHASE ONE

—

WHERE ARE WE NOW?

First things first. As your retreat gets underway, start with a time of prayer. In a spirit of humility, surrender to God and each other. Ask the Holy Spirit to guide you as you seek a vision for your marriage. Ask Him to build unity between you. Ask Him to refresh your souls.

## PREPARE

Plan to work together during your retreat. This is not a process that a single person, husband or wife, should control. You will be operating as a team. Be patient with each other and work to provide each other a safe place to share.

## WHAT ABOUT CONFLICT?

You will likely discuss some challenging issues during your retreat. These discussions might reveal areas in which the two of you disagree. That's not a bad thing! In fact, it's to be expected. Couples fight when they don't see eye-to-eye. They have different visions for their children, finances, priorities and more. If the two of you are not on the same page, then a vision retreat is exactly what you should be doing.

If conflict does occur, keep in mind Paul's words in Ephesians 4:26. He writes, "Be angry, and do not sin." There is nothing wrong with anger—even God gets angry— but don't use anger as a justification for bad behavior toward your spouse. Don't yell.

Don't curse. Don't accuse. Don't call names. And don't go to bed before resolving the issue. Going to bed without a resolution opens the door for you to lie in bed, angry at your spouse and stewing over your disagreement. That isn't healthy.

Instead, talk through your disagreements in a loving and positive manner. Explain your side of a conflict without criticizing your spouse. Then listen to your spouse's side and believe them. If you need to, forgive each other and try to move forward as God works on your hearts.

## COMMIT

Having prayed together and read through the previous paragraphs, are you both willing to commit to the process of seeking God together, speaking to each other with transparency and ultimately completing this guide? Then make it official.

_____   _____

Signature                         Date

_____   _____

Signature                         Date

## START POSITIVE

Pick someone to go first, then each of you take a moment to write down something positive your spouse has done for you in the past few days.

(HIM)

_____

_____

_____

_____

_____

_____

_____

(HER)

_____

_____

_____

_____

_____

_____

## PARENTING CHALLENGES

The next step is to take a snapshot of some of the issues you and your spouse may be dealing with. We'll start with parenting. Don't worry if the two of you are struggling as parents! You can have the world's best marriage and parenting will still be hard. Children will always push their boundaries.

When they do, it's important that the two of you agree with each other on consequences and discipline. Begin discussing how you can be more united on these issues. (If you can't resolve a situation right now, don't worry about it. But make sure each of you shares your individual perspective so you can start the conversation.)

| The Issue | Our United Response |
|---|---|
| *(Example Issue:* | *(Response:* |
| *"Daughter breaks curfew")* | *"Suspend driving privileges")* |
| _____ | _____ |
| _____ | _____ |
| _____ | _____ |
| _____ | _____ |

## FINANCIAL CHALLENGES

Money is a common source of disagreement in marriage. This happens because many individuals have different relationships to money. Take a moment to talk to your spouse about what money means to you. Does it mean security or does it mean freedom? Do you love to give it, spend it or save it? Does it cause you stress? Discuss these questions together:

(HIM) When I think about our finances I feel…

_____

_____

_____

My financial strengths are…

_____

_____

_____

My financial weaknesses are…

_____

_____

_____


(HER) When I think about our finances I feel…

_____

_____

_____


My financial strengths are…

_____

_____

_____


My financial weaknesses are…

_____

_____

_____


Now that you've discussed your individual feelings, strengths and weaknesses, take a look at the coming year. What types of financial decisions will you need to make? What challenges do you see coming? Discuss how you can work together to prepare for these.

| Potential Financial Challenges | We Will Prepare By... |
|---|---|
| _____ | _____ |
| _____ | _____ |
| _____ | _____ |
| _____ | _____ |

## RELATIONSHIP CHALLENGES

Men and women have different needs. Husbands tend to gravitate to the place where they are shown the most honor and respect. Women tend to gravitate toward the place where they feel the most security.

The best way to define these is to consider their absence. What does a marriage look like without honor or security? Imagine a husband who does not feel respected by his wife or family. She nags him. She gets angry and insults him. She ignores his input or constantly takes their children's side in disagreements. As a result, he feels emasculated, put upon, or even ignored. But in his career, the same husband is viewed as a leader and praised for his innovative thinking. That man will be drawn toward his business colleagues. He will pour his energy into his workplace because that's where he receives the most honor. At work he thrives, but his family and marriage suffer.

Likewise, most women seek security. Women feel most secure in a marriage to a sacrificial, sensitive man—a husband who willingly gives up his own interests for his family and who seeks to understand his wife's needs. But imagine a wife whose husband is selfish. He works hard all day, then comes home, sits in front of the TV, and ignores his family. He gets annoyed when his wife wants to talk about the children's schedules or the family's finances. He definitely doesn't want to discuss romance or spiritual matters. In this marriage, a woman will feel insecure due to her husband's lack of leadership and refusal to communicate. To meet that inner longing for security, she'll go looking for someone who makes her feel protected and provided for—and she may find it outside the marriage.

Many bad marriages start with a selfish, "out to lunch" man or an angry, dishonoring wife. Hopefully, these examples don't describe your marriage, but both of you will still have the need for honor (him) and security (her). Discuss what those needs look like for each of you.

(HIM)
Do you agree that honor and respect are important for a man?   YES   NO
Explain your answer.

_____

_____

_____

Tell your wife three or more ways she can show you honor and respect, then list them below.

_____

_____

_____

_____

_____

(HER)
Do you agree that security is important for a woman?   YES   NO
Explain your answer.

_____

_____

_____

Tell your husband three or more ways he can make you feel more loved and secure, then list them below.

_____

_____

_____

_____

_____

## PRIORITY AND SACRIFICE

One of the greatest ways we can show love to each other is through sacrifice—by giving up something of value in order to serve our spouse. Now that you've heard some of your spouse's needs, consider ways to make him or her a greater priority in the coming year. What might you be willing to sacrifice?

(HIM)
One way I can prioritize my wife this year is to...
_(Example: "...do more weekend activities together.")_

_____

_____

_____

To do so, I am willing to sacrifice...
_(Example: "...one round of golf every month.")_

_____

_____

_____

(HER)
One way I can prioritize my husband this year is to...
*(Example: "...show interest in one of his hobbies.")*

_____

_____

_____

To do so, I am willing to sacrifice...
*(Example: "...by making fewer Saturday appointments at the nail spa.")*

_____

_____

_____

# PHASE TWO

—

## WHERE ARE WE GOING?

---

*"When people do not accept divine guidance, they run wild.*
*But whoever obeys the law is joyful."*

PROVERBS 29:18 NLT

---

God has a purpose for your marriage. There is a reason He brought the two of you together! But to move forward in unity, you have to agree on your destination. Start this session in prayer, asking for His wisdom as you seek His plan and purpose. Consider praying something like this:

*Lord, we are so thankful for the time we have already spent together. Thank You for the conversations You are already using to bless our marriage. Please guide us as we continue talking. Give us ears to listen for Your direction. Give us hearts that are open to receiving it. Give us creativity as we plan, and honesty as we share our feelings. We are seeking Your will together, so guide us closer to each other as we draw closer to You. Amen.*

## FAMILY VISION

It's time to go deep! Together, discuss some of the purpose and principles guiding your relationship. These are hard questions, so talk about them together and then write down the answers.

What are some things God has called us to do together as a couple or family? (*Example: "To serve together in the church nursery" or "to volunteer at Grandmother's nursing home."*)

_____

_____

_____

_____

_____

Why did God put us together? (*Example: "To raise godly children who will have a positive impact on our community."*)

_____

_____

_____

_____

_____

When hard times come, how will our understanding of the purpose above impact our relationship? (*Example: "We will always keep in mind that we are modeling marriage for our kids."*)

_____

_____

_____

_____

_____

What has God called us to accomplish in the coming year to further His purpose?
*(Please answer as a couple and as individuals.)*

_____

_____

_____

_____

_____

As a couple:

_____

_____

_____

_____

Him:

_____

_____

_____

_____

Her:

_____

_____

_____

_____

Spoken or unspoken, every family has a "code"—a set of ethical or moral standards—that they live by. Discuss what you want these to be within your family, then list them. (*Example: "We always do the right thing, even when it's also the hardest thing."*)

1. _____

2. _____

3. _____

4. _____

5. _____


If someone were describing your marriage, what words would you want them to use? (*Examples: Inspiring, Fun, Positive, Encouraging, Hopeful, Solid...*)

1. _____

2. _____

3. _____

4. _____

5. _____


## FAMILY VALUES

Individuals have core values and principles. These are the driving force behind the decisions we make and the actions we take. Because a marriage is made from the union of two individuals, it also should be guided by a set of dreams, values and beliefs. Unless the two of you walk in agreement on these, you won't make progress in any direction. Discuss these core values with each other.

What are the most deeply held beliefs or values in our family?
(*Example: "Jesus is the hope the world needs" or "Treat everyone with kindness."*)

_____

_____

_____

_____

_____

In what ways does our family excel? List your family's passions or giftings. (*Example: "We are great at making others feel welcome in our home."*)

_____

_____

_____

_____

What are the sources of stress in our family or our family's schedule? How can we lower or limit that stress?

| **Sources of Stress** | **How We Can Limit Stress** |
|---|---|
| (*Example: "Overly busy schedules"*) | (*Example: "No Sunday activities other than church"*) |
| _____ | _____ |
| _____ | _____ |
| _____ | _____ |
| _____ | _____ |

Each of you list three ways you would want someone to describe the atmosphere of your home or family.

Him: *(Example: "Always there for each other.")*

1. _____

2. _____

3. _____

Her: *(Example: "Kind and loving.")*

1. _____

2. _____

3. _____

Are there any specific changes you can make to cultivate that atmosphere in your family? Discuss with each other and then, if necessary, write them down here. *(Example: "Talk more often with our kids about the things we value and the kind of people we want to be. Look for teachable opportunities.")*

_____

_____

_____

_____

_____

_____

## CHILDREN & GRANDCHILDREN

If the two of you have children together, raising them will take up significant space within your marriage until they are grown. During this period, don't ever let your children divide you. It's critical that the two of you get on the same page when it comes to values, activities, discipline and more! In a healthy marriage, the husband and wife present a united front to their children. Spend time talking about your roles as parents.

How can we transmit our beliefs or values to our children?
(Example: "Be intentional. Talk regularly. Don't assume they'll learn everything from osmosis.")

_____

_____

_____

_____

_____

_____

When our children are grown, what kinds of memories of family life do we want them to hold dear? What specifically do we need to change, add to or eliminate from our lives in order to produce those memories?
(Example: "We want them to remember our home as a safe, happy place. We need to praise them and compliment each other more often in front of them.")

_____

_____

_____

_____

When it comes to spiritual development and religious beliefs, what would we like to teach our children?
(*Example: "We want to teach them that prayer is effective, and to always pray for each other—and for us."*)

_____

_____

_____

_____

What should discipline look like as we parent together? How can we correct our children while still showing love and protecting their self-esteem?
(*Example: "Phone use requires trust. It is a privilege. If not used according to our rules, we can remove that privilege."*)

_____

_____

_____

_____

Unity is essential in parenting. In terms of discipline and correction, how can we operate as a team? How do we keep from undermining one another in applying correction?
(*Example: "We never make a unilateral decision about punishments. We always discuss specific discipline together before communicating to a child."*)

_____

_____

_____

_____

# PHASE THREE

—

## WHAT WILL WE DO?

*"Write the vision and make it plain on tablets,
that he may run who reads it."*

HABAKKUK 2:2 NKJV

If you're ready for a marriage that sprints in a healthy, hopeful direction, it's time to write down your goals. Retreat conversations like you've already had are deeply beneficial, but this next step—spelling out your vision—adds motivation. It keeps the goal in front of you during the months to come. It propels you toward fulfilling your purpose.

So with God's help, use this section to detail the results of your conversations and the specific goals and visions God has placed before you. Then return to these pages throughout the year.

## THE SPIRITUAL LIFE OF OUR FAMILY AND/OR MARRIAGE

Vision/Goals:

*(Example: "Constantly seek God's will for our marriage and family.")*

_____

_____

_____

_____

_____

Actions to take:

*(Example: "Pray together every night before bed.")*

_____

_____

_____

_____

_____

## OUR SPIRITUAL LIVES AS INDIVIDUALS

His goals:

*(Example: "Spend more time reading the Bible or devotional books.")*

_____

_____

_____

_____

_____

His actions to take:

*(Example: "Start every weekday with a 15-minute, personal devotional time.")*

_____

_____

_____

_____

Her goals:

_____

_____

_____

_____

_____

Her actions to take:

_____

_____

_____

_____

_____

## SERVING OTHERS TOGETHER
Vision/Goals:
*(Example: "Volunteer more in our community.")*

_____

_____

_____

_____

_____

Actions to take:

*(Example: "Get connected with the adult literacy council. Serve there 3-4 hours per month.")*

_____

_____

_____

_____

_____

## ROMANCE AND SEXUAL INTIMACY

Vision/Goals:

*(Example: "Improve our sex life.")*

_____

_____

_____

_____

_____

Actions to take:

*(Example: "Schedule sex? For the next six months, we'll have sex every Friday night!")*

_____

_____

_____

_____

_____

## FINANCES

Vision/Goals:

*(Example: "Build up an emergency fund equivalent to two months of income.")*

_____

_____

_____

_____

_____

Actions to take:

*(Example: "Set up automatic transfer of $200/month to savings.")*

_____

_____

_____

_____

_____

## WORK AND CAREER

His goals:

_____

_____

His actions to take:

_____

_____

Her goals:

_____

_____

Her actions to take:

_____

_____

## FAMILY CULTURE AND HOME LIFE

Vision/Goals:

*(Example: "Eat together more often as a family.")*

_____

_____

_____

_____

_____

Actions to take:

*(Example: "Put it on our calendars: Thursday night is always family dinner night.")*

_____

_____

_____

_____

## EXTENDED FAMILY RELATIONSHIPS

Vision/Goals:

*(Example: "Make sure our kids develop relationships with their grandparents.")*

_____

_____

_____

_____

_____

Actions to take:

*(Example: "Talk to Grandma and PawPaw about a weekly Facetime session.")*

_____

_____

_____

_____

_____

## FRIENDSHIPS

Vision/Goals:

*(Example: "Work on developing positive friendships with other couples our age.")*

_____

_____

_____

_____

Actions to take:
*(Example: "Ask friends about starting a supper club.")*

_____

_____

_____

_____

**HEALTH**
His goals:
*(Example: "Lose 15 pounds this year.")*

_____

_____

_____

His actions to take:
*(Example: "Take a 20-minute walk around the park together every night after dinner.")*

_____

_____

_____

Her goals:
*(Example: "Improve our family's overall diet.")*

_____

_____

_____

Her actions to take:
(Example: "Find recipes using fresh ingredients. Prepare food at home one additional night per week.")

_____

_____

_____

## OUR CHILDREN

List each child (or grandchild) by name. Then write your dream for them, your prayer for them, and how you can work within God's plan to help fulfill that prayer.

**Child's name:** _____

Dream:
(*Example: "That she'll be a strong, confident woman of faith."*)

_____

_____

_____

Prayer:
(*Example: "Lord, help our daughter know your love and have the courage to stand up for herself and her friends this year at school."*)

_____

_____

_____

Our role:

*(Example: "Weekly check-in about social media use, relationship drama and any other issues in her friend group.")*

_____

_____

_____

**Child's name:** _____

Dream:

_____

_____

_____

Prayer:

_____

_____

_____

Our role:

_____

_____

_____

**Child's name:** _____

Dream:

_____

_____

_____

Prayer:

_____

_____

_____

Our role:

_____

_____

_____

**Child's name:** _____

Dream:

_____

_____

_____

Prayer:

_____

_____

_____

Our role:

_____

_____

_____

**Child's name:** _____

Dream:

_____

_____

_____

Prayer:

_____

_____

_____

Our role:

_____

_____

_____

## OTHER
Vision/Goals:

_____

_____

_____

_____

_____

_____

Actions to take:

_____

_____

_____

_____

_____

_____

## OTHER

(Use this section if you need additional space for any of the goals/actions above, or if you wish to establish goals for anything not listed already.)

Vision/Goals:

_____

_____

_____

Actions to take:

_____

_____

_____

Vision/Goals:

_____

_____

_____

Actions to take:

_____

_____

_____

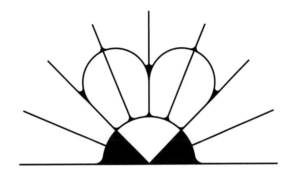

# PHASE FOUR

---

## A VISION FOR OUR
## MARRIAGE AND FAMILY

*"When two people are together in any endeavor in life, it is only possible for them to remain unified and productive if they both share the same vision and purpose. Therefore, it is of paramount importance that every couple hoping to succeed take the time and energy to get God's vision for their marriage."*

JIMMY EVANS

Congratulations! You've reached the final phase of your retreat. This last section is the culmination of everything you've been discussing and dreaming together. Take everything you've learned and recorded in this guide and use it to create an overall vision statement for your family.

Some instructions as you craft this vision:

1. **Pray.** Ask God to guide you as you develop your vision statement.
2. **Dream.** Ask each other: What words do we want people to use when they describe our family?
3. **Consider.** Your vision should include every part of your life, including spiritual, relational, personal, family (parental) and financial categories.
4. **Balance.** It should represent both spouses' individual perspectives and most cherished beliefs.
5. **Review.** Look at your answers to all the previous questions and prompts. Are there any key themes that stand out? Include those in your vision statement.
6. **Simplify.** The best vision statements are short and to the point. Consider coming up with a motto or acronym to help you remember it.
7. **Scripture.** Is there a Bible verse or passage that applies? If so, note it and include it.

## THE SUMMARY OF OUR VISION

Date: _____

**Overall Vision:**
*(Keep your summary statement short but well-defined. Example: "We strive to be a couple that prays together regularly, communicates clearly, makes sacrifices for one another, prioritizes church attendance, and looks for practical ways to love those around us. In our marriage, we will honor and serve God while honoring and serving each other to the best of our abilities.")*

_____

_____

_____

_____

_____

_____

_____

_____

**Key Scripture(s):**

_____

_____

_____

_____

**Optional: Include further details about these specific categories.**

_____

_____

_____

_____

_____

## Our Spiritual Lives

(Example: "Going forward, wherever we live, we will become members of a nearby church and attend faithfully. We will tithe, participate in worship, and serve when possible. We will pray daily and talk about what God is doing in our lives on a regular basis.")

_____

_____

_____

_____

_____

## Our Relationship

(Example: "We believe the best marriage starts with two servants in love, so we will lovingly serve and sacrifice for each other. Every day, we will set aside time—apart from the kids—to talk about our day. We refuse to go to bed angry.")

_____

_____

_____

_____

_____

## Our Family

*(Example: "We will raise our children to serve God and show kindness to others. Volunteering is one of our core values, so our family will try to give back at least two hours a month at a local nonprofit. We will value talking or playing together over watching TV.")*

_____

_____

_____

_____

_____

## Our Finances

*(Example: "Every month, we will donate 10% of our income to our church and try to save another 10% to build an emergency fund. We will prioritize avoiding debt and will only use credit cards wisely.")*

_____

_____

_____

_____

_____

_____

## Other Specifics

_____

_____

_____

_____

_____

_____

_____

_____

_____

_____

_____

_____

_____

_____

_____

_____

# NEXT STEPS

## Do It Again

You're finished! Congratulations on putting in this hard work on behalf of your marriage. Over the course of the next year, we believe this process will bring the two of you closer than ever before. As a last step, turn back to page XVIII.

You each rated the intimacy of your marriage before starting this retreat process. Where is your marriage right now? Take a moment to re-evaluate your closeness.

HIM: Now that we are almost finished, I rate the intimacy and closeness of our marriage as…

**Less Intimate**                                                 **More Intimate**

   1       2       3       4       5       6       7       8       9     10

HER: Now that we are almost finished, I rate the intimacy and closeness of our marriage as…

**Less Intimate**                                                                          **More Intimate**

1        2        3        4        5        6        7        8        9        10

Hopefully, you are closer now than you were at the beginning of this journey. Every time you go through a vision retreat, it will take your marriage to the next level. So don't just do it once! Do it again, year after year. When you do, it will not only help remind you of who you are and what you're trying to accomplish, but it will continue to spur growth, intimacy and commitment. You'll see God bless your relationship like never before.

As you go home and start your lives with this vision, continue talking. Discuss these things on your date nights. Remind yourself of these goals regularly. Don't stop praying for each other. Track your progress and celebrate your victories.

Before you put this book down, pray one more time. Thank God for what he has shown you. Thank Him for each other. Recommit to your marriage.
Then make plans to do this again next year.

# JIMMY & KAREN EVANS

*"Karen and I had our first Vision Retreat more than 25 years ago, and it just changed everything. It changes your family for generations."*

JIMMY EVANS

"Pack your bags and get out of this house and my life!" When Jimmy Evans found himself saying those harsh words to his wife, Karen, he knew something had to change. She was sobbing. He was stubborn. Both found themselves somewhere they never expected to be: on the brink of divorce.

Separately, both began to pray. Karen prayed for her husband. Jimmy asked God for help. Soon, the Holy Spirit breathed conviction and hope into their marriage. Both Jimmy and Karen sought forgiveness for their sin, asking for an outpouring of the limitless mercy of God.

Together, the two of them dove into God's Word and began a journey of discovery. They applied the biblical principles they learned and established a much stronger foundation for their marriage. Their relationship began to grow and flourish. Soon, they found their marriage in an unfamiliar place. It had become healthy. It was strong. It was romantic.

They had discovered paradise—together.

Now, through XO Marriage, they teach other couples how to find success in marriage. Today they can say with all confidence, "Your family has a great future!" God did it for them. They know He can and will do it for you.

Find more resources for strengthening and enriching your marriage at xomarriage.com.